ALL
YOU
NEED
IS
LOVE

ALL YOU NEED IS LOVE ALL YOU NEED IS LOVE ALL YOU NEED IS LOVE ALL YOU NEED IS LOVE

ALL YOU NEED IS LOVE ALL YOU NEED IS LOVE ALL YOU NEED IS LOVE AL YOU NEE IS LOVE

ALL YOU NEED IS LOVE ALL YOU NEED IS LOVE ALL YOU NEED IS LOVE ALL YOU NEED IS LOVE

ALL YOU NEED IS LOVE ALL YOU NEED IS LOVE ALL YOU NEED IS LOVE AL YOU NEE IS LOVE

ALL
YOU
NEED
IS
LOVE

summersdale

ALL YOU NEED IS LOVE

Summersdale Publishers Ltd
46 West Street
Chichester
West Sussex
PO19 1RP
UK

www.summersdale.com

Printed and bound in the Czech Republic

ISBN: 978-1-84953-130-6

Substantial discounts on bulk quantities of Summersdale books are available to corporations, professional associations and other organisations. For details contact Summersdale Publishers by telephone: +44 (0) 1243 771107, fax: +44 (0) 1243 786300 or email: nicky@summersdale.com.

ALL
YOU
NEED
IS
LOVE

The best thing to hold
onto in life is
each other.

Audrey Hepburn

What the world really needs
is more love and less
paperwork.

Pearl Bailey

The more I think it over,
the more I feel that there is
nothing more truly artistic
than to love people.

Vincent Van Gogh

I am in love – and, my
God, it's the greatest
thing that can happen
to a man.

D. H. Lawrence

Love is the answer, but while you're waiting for the answer, sex raises some pretty good questions.

Woody Allen

The war between the sexes is the only one in which both sides regularly sleep with the enemy.

Quentin Crisp

Where there is love
there is no question.

Albert Einstein

If grass can grow through cement, love can find you at every time in your life.

Cher

Every time we love,
every time we give,
it's Christmas.

Dale Evans

If love is blind, why is
lingerie so popular?

Anonymous

In the Spring a young
man's fancy lightly turns to
thoughts of love.

**Alfred, Lord Tennyson,
'Locksley Hall'**

Love: a temporary
insanity, curable
by marriage.

Ambrose Bierce,
The Devil's Dictionary

In love the paradox occurs that two beings become one and yet remain two.

Erich Fromm

I like to believe that love is a reciprocal thing, that it can't really be felt, truly, by one.

Sean Penn

A kiss is a lovely trick
designed by nature to stop
speech when words become
superfluous.

Ingrid Bergman

Love's like the measles – all the worse when it comes late in life.

Douglas Jerrold

Three things can't be
hidden: coughing, poverty
and love.

Yiddish proverb

Sometimes the heart
sees what is invisible
to the eye.

H. Jackson Brown Jr

Love is like smiling; it never fades and is contagious.

Paula Deen

Anyone can be passionate,
but it takes real lovers
to be silly.

Rose Franken

To fall in love you have to be in the state of mind for it to take, like a disease.

Nancy Mitford

Love is not the dying moan
of a distant violin – it's the
triumphant twang of
a bedspring.

S. J. Perelman

It is impossible to love
and be wise.

Francis Bacon, 'Of Love'

I married the first man I ever kissed. When I tell my children that they just about throw up.

Barbara Bush

Love is an irresistible
desire to be irresistibly
desired.

Robert Frost

There is only one happiness
in life: to love and be loved.

George Sand

Never go to bed mad.
Stay up and fight.

Phyllis Diller

A man is already halfway in love with any woman who listens to him.

Brendan Francis

In love there are two things:
bodies and words.

Joyce Carol Oates

Love is a grave
mental disease.

Plato

The only creatures
that are evolved
enough to convey
pure love are dogs
and infants.

Johnny Depp

Do you want me to tell you something really subversive? Love is everything it's cracked up to be.

Erica Jong,
How to Save Your Own Life

A heart that loves is
always young.

Greek proverb

Women marry men hoping they will change. Men marry women hoping they will not. So each is inevitably disappointed.

Albert Einstein

Forget love, I'd rather fall in chocolate.

Sandra J. Dykes

Marriage is a romance in
which the heroine dies in the
first chapter.

Cecilia Egan

I have spread my dreams
under your feet;
Tread softly because you
tread on my dreams.

**William Butler Yeats, 'He Wishes
for the Cloths of Heaven'**

To be in love is merely to be in a state of perpetual anaesthesia.

H. L. Mencken

The trouble with some women is that they get all excited about nothing – and then marry him.

Cher

Love does not consist in gazing at each other but in looking in the same direction.

Antoine de Saint-Exupéry

Love is blind –
marriage is the
eye-opener.

Pauline Thomason

I never hated a man enough
to give him his diamonds
back.

Zsa Zsa Gabor

If you really love someone
and care about him, you can
survive many difficulties.

Calvin Klein

Love can turn the
cottage into a golden
palace.

German proverb

Romance cannot
be put into quantity
production – the
moment love becomes
casual, it becomes
commonplace.

Frederick Lewis Allen,
Only Yesterday

I'm tired of Love: I'm still
more tired of Rhyme.
But Money gives me
pleasure all the time.

Hilaire Belloc

Falling in love consists merely in uncorking the imagination and bottling the common sense.

Helen Rowland

Love is like dew that
falls on both nettles
and lilies.

Swedish proverb

When a man steals your
wife there is no better
revenge than to let him
keep her.

Sacha Guitry

What would men
be without women?
Scarce, sir, mighty
scarce.

Mark Twain

Love is not altogether a
delirium, yet it has many
points in common therewith.

Thomas Carlyle

What force is more
potent than love?

Igor Stravinsky

Many a young lady does not realise just how strong her love for a young man is until he fails to pass the approval test with her parents.

Anonymous

The course of true
love never did
run smooth.

William Shakespeare,
A Midsummer Night's Dream

When you are in love you can't fall asleep because reality is better than your dreams.

Dr Seuss

There is a time for work. And a time for love. That leaves no other time.

Coco Chanel

Where love is concerned,
too much is not
even enough.

Pierre de Beaumarchais

To fall in love is to
create a religion that
has a fallible god.

**Jorge Luis Borges,
'The Meeting in a Dream'**

There's only two people in
your life you should lie to…
the police and your girlfriend.

Jack Nicholson

It was a perfect marriage. She didn't want to and he couldn't.

Spike Milligan

A life without love is like a year without summer.

Swedish proverb

You come to love not by
finding the perfect person,
but by seeing an imperfect
person perfectly.

Sam Keen

Platonic love is love
from the neck up.

Thyra Samter Winslow

The quickest way to a man's
heart is through his chest.

Roseanne Barr

If I know what love is,
it is because of you.

Herman Hesse

Kiss me and you will see
how important I am.

Sylvia Plath

True love comes quietly, without banners or flashing lights. If you hear bells, get your ears checked.

Erich Segal

Bigamy is having
one wife too many.
Monogamy is
the same.

Oscar Wilde

Love is a friendship
set to music.

Eli Joseph Cossman

You're in love. That makes
you actually kind of boring
to people who aren't in love.

Claudia Gray

When I eventually met
Mr Right I had no idea
that his first name
was Always.

Rita Rudner

My wife always said a good meal and a good tango are enough to make you happy. She's right.

Robert Duvall

The tragedy of love
is indifference.

W. Somerset Maugham,
The Trembling of a Leaf

I've been married so long
I'm on my third bottle of
Tabasco sauce.

Susan Vass

In love, the one who
runs away is
the winner.

Henri Matisse

I haven't spoken to my wife
in years. I didn't want to
interrupt her.

Rodney Dangerfield

To love and win is the best thing. To love and lose, the next best.

William Makepeace Thackeray,
The History of Pendennis

Marriage is like putting your
hand into a bag of snakes in
the hope of pulling
out an eel.

Leonardo da Vinci

Love is an exploding
cigar we willingly
smoke.

Lynda Barry

The art of love… is largely
the art of persistence.

Albert Ellis

A man falls in love
through his eyes,
a woman through
her ears.

Woodrow Wyatt

Marriage is a great
institution, but I'm not ready
for an institution yet.

Mae West

Twenty years of romance
make a woman look like
a ruin; but twenty years
of marriage make her
something like a
public building.

Oscar Wilde,
A Woman of No Importance

Love is not
consolation.
It is light.

Friedrich Nietzsche

Love is the self-delusion we manufacture to justify the trouble we take to have sex.

Dan Greenburg

No job is as important
to me as my love.

Jennifer Aniston

It's easy to fall in love. The
hard part is finding someone
to catch you.

Bertrand Russell

Strong women leave
big hickies.

Madonna

On stage, I make love to
25,000 different people,
then I go home alone.

Janis Joplin

Lust is easy. Love is hard. Like is most important.

Carl Reiner

I'm blessed to have a
husband who walks through
the door and looks at me
like every day's Christmas.

Kate Beckinsale

When I saw you I
fell in love. And you
smiled because
you knew.

Arrigo Boito

A pair of powerful
spectacles has sometimes
sufficed to cure a person
in love.

Friedrich Nietzsche

Love is the joy of the
good, the wonder
of the wise, the
amazement of
the Gods.

Plato

A deal is a deal. To me, that just says it all. Marriage is for keeps.

Courtney Cox Arquette

When you love someone, all
your saved-up wishes start
coming out.

Elizabeth Bowen

A wise girl kisses but
doesn't love, listens but
doesn't believe, and leaves
before she is left.

Marilyn Monroe

And yet, to say the truth, reason and love keep little company together nowadays.

William Shakespeare,
A Midsummer Night's Dream

Love conquers all
things; let us too
surrender to love.

Virgil, *Eclogues*

I love Mickey Mouse more
than any woman I have
ever known.

Walt Disney

Love and war are the same
thing, and stratagems and
policy are as allowable in
the one as in the other.

Miguel de Cervantes, *Don Quixote*

Some women choose
to follow men, and
some women choose
to follow their dreams.

Lady Gaga

I really think that all men should celebrate their women… They should all jump on couches for them.

Tom Cruise on his relationship with Katie Holmes

Many a good hanging
prevents a bad
marriage.

William Shakespeare, *Twelfth Night*

You don't have to be singing
about love all the time in
order to give love to
the people.

Jimi Hendrix

You can't put a price tag on love, but you can on all its accessories.

Melanie Clark

Laugh and the world laughs with you, snore and you sleep alone.

Anthony Burgess

Love is an indescribable
sensation – perhaps a
conviction, a sense
of certitude.

Joyce Carol Oates

No love is entirely without worth, even when the frivolous calls to the frivolous and the base to the base.

Iris Murdoch,
The Nice and the Good

Marriage isn't a
word… it's a sentence!

King Vidor

One of the secrets of life is
that all that is really worth
the doing is what we do
for others.

Lewis Carroll

I change my mind
so much I need two
boyfriends and
a girlfriend.

Pink

It is a woman's business to get married as soon as possible, and a man's to keep unmarried for as long as possible.

George Bernard Shaw,
Man and Superman

When we are in love
we seem to ourselves
quite different from
what we were before.

Blaise Pascal

My wife and I tried to breakfast together, but we had to stop or our marriage would have been wrecked.

Winston Churchill

Love is composed of a single soul inhabiting two bodies.

Aristotle

I like to wake up each
morning feeling a
new man.

Jean Harlow

The best way to get
husbands to do something
is to suggest that… they are
too old to do it.

Shirley MacLaine

One word frees us of
all the weight and pain
of life: that word
is love.

Sophocles

Marriage is a very good thing, but I think it's a mistake to make a habit out of it.

W. Somerset Maugham, 'The Treasure'

The only thing worse than
a man you can't control is a
man you can.

Margo Kaufman

Love is being
stupid together.

Paul Valéry

There are two
perfectly good men,
one dead, and the
other unborn.

Chinese proverb

How often do I have sex?
Those who count clearly
aren't enjoying it enough.

Nick Clegg

Love is a canvas
furnished by nature
and embroidered by
the imagination.

Voltaire

Bachelors know more about women than married men; if they didn't they'd be married too.

H. L. Mencken

Your words are my food,
your breath my wine. You
are everything to me.

Sarah Bernhardt

Don't let love interfere with your appetite. It never does with mine.

Anthony Trollope,
Barchester Towers

Love at first sight?
I absolutely believe in it!
You've got to keep the faith.

Leonardo DiCaprio

Next to being married,
a girl likes to be
crossed in love a little
now and then.

Jane Austen, *Pride and Prejudice*

Trouble is, by the time you
can read a girl like a book,
your library card
has expired.

Milton Berle

Love is an electric
blanket with
somebody else in
control of the switch.

Cathy Carlyle

I want to do with you what
spring does with
cherry trees.

Pablo Neruda

Marriage is a dinner
that begins with
dessert.

Henri de Toulouse-Lautrec

He that falls in love
with himself will have
no rivals.

Benjamin Franklin

A man is as good as he has
to be, and a woman as bad
as she dares.

Elbert Hubbard

To love is to receive a glimpse of heaven.

Karen Sunde

Love conquers all things
except poverty and
toothache.

Mae West

'Tis better to have loved
and lost
Than never to have loved
at all.

**Alfred, Lord Tennyson,
'In Memoriam'**

A historical romance is
the only kind of book
where chastity
really counts.

Barbara Cartland

All love is original,
no matter how many
other people have
loved before.

George Weinberg

Make love to every woman
you meet; if you get five
per cent of your outlay it's a
good investment.

Arnold Bennett

We love because
it's the only true
adventure.

Nikki Giovanni

I have great hopes that we shall love each other all our lives as much as if we had never married at all.

Lord Byron

Bisexuality doubles your chances of a date on a Saturday night.

Woody Allen

Love is like pi –
natural, irrational and
very important.

Lisa Hoffman

As the arteries grow
hard, the heart
grows soft.

H. L. Mencken

To love and be loved is to
feel the sun from both sides.

David Viscott

Marriage may often be a stormy lake, but celibacy is almost always a muddy horsepond.

Thomas Love Peacock,
Melincourt

A man in love is incomplete until he is married. Then he's finished.

Zsa Zsa Gabor

The magic of first love is our
ignorance that it can
ever end.

Benjamin Disraeli

Real love stories
never have endings.

Richard Bach

KEEP
CALM
AND
DRINK
UP

KEEP CALM AND DRINK UP

£4.99

ISBN: 978 1 84953 102 3

'*In victory, you deserve champagne;
in defeat, you need it.*'

Napoleon Bonaparte

BAD ADVICE FOR GOOD PEOPLE.

Keep Calm and Carry On, a World War Two government poster, struck a chord in recent difficult times when a stiff upper lip and optimistic energy were needed again. But in the long run it's a stiff drink and flowing spirits that keep us all going.

Here's a book packed with proverbs and quotations showing the wisdom to be found at the bottom of the glass.

NOW
PANIC
AND
FREAK
OUT

NOW PANIC AND FREAK OUT

£4.99

ISBN: 978 1 84953 103 0

'*We experience moments absolutely free from worry. These brief respites are called panic.*'

Cullen Hightower

BAD ADVICE FOR GOOD PEOPLE.

Keep Calm and Carry On is all very well, but life just isn't that simple. Let's own up and face facts: we're getting older, the politicians are not getting any wiser, and the world's going to hell in a handbasket.

It's time to panic.

Here's a book packed with quotations proving that keeping calm is simply not an option.

www.summersdale.com

ALL YOU NEED IS LOVE

ALL YOU NEED IS LOVE
ALL YOU NEED IS LOVE
ALL YOU NEED IS LOVE
ALL YOU NEED IS LOVE
ALL YOU NEED IS LOVE
ALL YOU NEED IS LOVE
ALL YOU NEED IS LOVE

ALL ALL ALL ALL
YOU YOU YOU YOU
EED NEED NEED NEED
S IS IS IS
VE LOVE LOVE LOVE

ALL ALL ALL ALL
YOU YOU YOU YOU
NEED NEED NEED NEED
IS IS IS IS
OVE LOVE LOVE LOVE

ALL ALL ALL ALL
YOU YOU YOU YOU
EED NEED NEED NEED
S IS IS IS
VE LOVE LOVE LOVE

ALL ALL ALL ALL
YOU YOU YOU YOU
NEED NEED NEED NEED
IS IS IS IS
OVE LOVE LOVE LOVE